WORLD IN  DANGER

WILDLIFE

Steve Pollock
Illustrated by Peter Wingham

Belitha Press

First published in Great Britain in 1990 by
Belitha Press Limited
31 Newington Green, London N16 9PU

Text copyright © Steve Pollock 1990
Illustrations copyright © Peter Wingham 1990
Editor: Neil Champion

ISBN 1-85561-007-8 (hardback)
ISBN 1-85561-027-2 (paperback)

Printed in the UK by MacLehose For Imago Publishing
Printed on recycled paper (135 gsm Envirocote)

Contents

Why we need wildlife

Our world is a living world, full of millions of different kinds of plants and animals. They all depend on each other in some way. Can you think of some ways in which you depend on plants and animals?

The different kinds of plants and animals are like a pile of building blocks, all carefully balanced on top of each other. Pull some of the blocks away and what happens? The pile collapses!

When people damage the **environment** or destroy wildlife, they are pulling

Some plants and animals that help cure diseases

away the building blocks of nature. People, like you and me, are a part of nature so taking out the blocks will harm us as well.

Let's look at why we need wildlife. All the food we eat comes from plants and animals. Most modern types are descended from wild varieties. Did you know that chickens are descended from the Indian red jungle fowl? Plants and animals also give us **medicines**

Wildlife gives us enjoyment

to help us keep healthy. Plants and animals are important to us in lots of other ways too. But even if they weren't, don't you think they have a right to be here?

Catching frogs

Plants and animals have always been important to people as food. However, some people have tried to make money from selling animals as special **delicacies** to those who could afford them. This can lead to problems.

Here is a true story about how killing wildlife for food made people go hungry. People like eating frog's legs as an expensive delicacy.
So someone had a bright idea – why not catch the thousands of bullfrogs

that live in India's wet rice fields, and sell their legs to shops and restaurants?

So people were sent out to catch the frogs. The people that caught them were pleased with the extra money they

earned. People in restaurants all over the world could now eat their favourite

delicacy again. Everybody was happy, except the bullfrogs, of course.

But before long disaster struck. The rice **crop** failed, so the people had to spend all their extra money, and more, on food. What had happened to the rice? The bullfrogs used to eat the insects that damage the rice crop. Without the frogs, the insects multiplied out of control, and ruined all the rice plants.

By interfering with nature, it is easy to upset its delicate balance. It is much harder to put things right again.

Extinction is forever

We use the word "**extinct**" for plants and animals that have completely died out, or all been killed – like the dinosaurs. We don't know how they went extinct, but it was not because of people, because there were no people at the time. But people have made many other animals (and plants) extinct.

The dodo is famous for this reason. It was a large flightless bird that lived on the island of Mauritius in the Indian Ocean. During the 17th century, Mauritius was visited by European sailors. They killed and ate the dodos. They also left pigs behind to eat on their next visit.

The pigs ate the dodos' eggs and by 1693 there were no dodos. We still use the expression "dead as a dodo".

People are still destroying wildlife without learning from the past or thinking about the future.

Hunting

Most people today do not need to hunt, as their food is grown on farms. In the USA some people dig up rare desert **cacti** to sell to collectors all over the world. This is **illegal**, but there is a lot of money to be made, so it still goes on.

People who hunt illegally are called **poachers**.

All rhinoceroses are protected, yet poachers still kill them for their horns. Some people think rhino horn is a strong medicine. But rhino horn is made from the same stuff as our fingernails! Of course, it does nothing special at all.

People do not always realise that it can be illegal to travel from country to country with things made from plants and animals. They can end up having their things taken by **customs** officers.

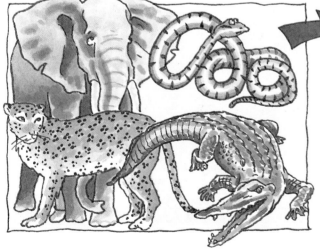

Many kinds of **reptiles** such as snakes, crocodiles, lizards and alligators are killed and their skins made into shoes, handbags, wallets and belts.

Do people really look good wearing other animals' skins?

Habitat destruction

Every kind of plant or animal lives in a particular environment, which it shares with others. This is its habitat. When a habitat is destroyed, all its wildlife is destroyed at the same time, so this is perhaps the worst way we put wildlife in danger.

Some habitats, like tropical rainforests, are being pulled down, making many plants and animals extinct.

Wetlands, which are valuable for wildlife, are being drained to make way for buildings and farmland. In Britain, ponds are filled to make fields bigger,

leaving frogs, newts and other animals with nowhere to live or breed.

Where there was a pond, now there is a road.

Huge dams are flooding thousands of square kilometres, drowning fields, villages, forests and wildlife.

Few plants and animals can survive or adapt to these sudden, drastic changes.

Pollution

One way in which we are harming wildlife is by **pollution** – putting poisonous or dangerous stuff into the environment. One example is the smoke from car exhausts and from the tall chimneys on factories and power stations. The gases in the smoke mix with the air and clouds to make acids which come back down in the rain. The **acid rain** can kill trees and fish.

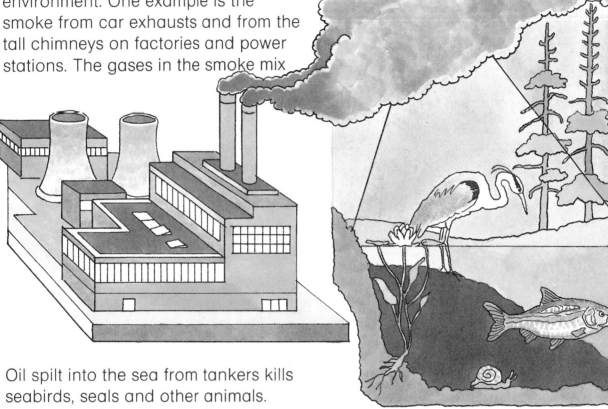

Oil spilt into the sea from tankers kills seabirds, seals and other animals. Once fur or feathers are clogged up with oil, they no longer keep out the cold, so animals die of cold!

Perhaps the worst pollution is from poisonous chemicals. Some of these are so poisonous that even a tiny bit is very dangerous, like some chemicals that were used by farmers in the USA to kill insect pests. Some of the chemicals

got washed into the mud along the seaside, where they worked their way into tiny animals. The fish ate the tiny

animals, then ospreys (a bird of prey) ate the fish. Eating more fish meant eating more chemicals. When the ospreys had too much of the chemicals in them, their egg shells came out so thin, that the eggs broke before the chicks hatched. Because of this, the ospreys nearly died out. The chemicals were banned and the ospreys have returned.

Saving the animals

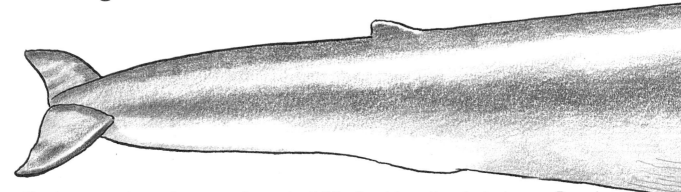

There was a time when people and wildlife lived together in balance. People would only kill the animals they needed for food, and leave the rest for another day. Now we have destroyed that balance by taking too much. This is the story of how we mistreated just two of the world's animals, and brought them both to the brink of extinction.

People hunted blue whales for their meat, bone and valuable oils. In the early days, hunting whales was a difficult and dangerous job. Only a few whales could be killed, so there were always plenty left.

Then people started using fast, modern ships with exploding harpoons to kill the whales more quickly. In 1930 nearly 30,000 blue whales were killed. In no time at

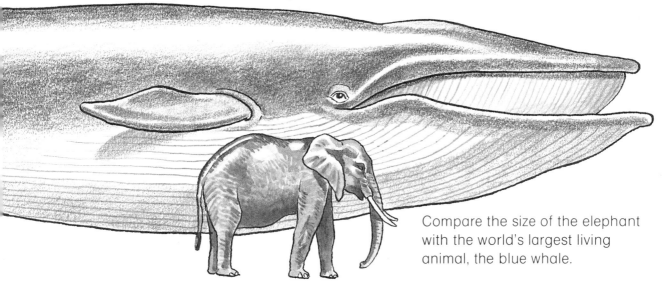

Compare the size of the elephant with the world's largest living animal, the blue whale.

all there were so few blue whales left that it was hardly worth hunting them. Only then was the blue whale made a protected species.

Before white people settled in North America, as many as sixty million bison lived there. Once people from Europe started to live there, the numbers dropped. Nearly every bison was killed as the white pioneers moved across the country. The last few were thankfully saved and today they live in protected areas.

National parks

One good way to save wildlife is to make protected areas, like the Serengeti National Park in Tanzania, Africa. Here, thousands of wild animals including lions, antelopes, zebras, leopards, elephants and buffaloes all live together, watched by game wardens and tourists from around the world.

Even in a national park the animals are not always safe. Poachers hunt the elephants for their tusks, and the rhinoceroses for their horns. Game

wardens risk fighting with the poachers and maybe getting killed themselves.

As more people use land, there will be fewer places for wildlife to live safely, making protected areas even more important for the future.

The picture above shows some of the things that might be going on right now in the Serengeti National Park. See if you can recognise the animals living there and work out what is happening.

Captive breeding

Another way to save animals from extinction is to keep them in zoos or wildlife parks, where they can breed safely. When there are enough of them, they can be returned to the wild.

The Brazilian golden lion marmoset, a kind of monkey, nearly went extinct because so much of the forest it lived in had been destroyed. So zoos all over the world started breeding their golden lion marmosets. Now there are so many that they are releasing them back into the wild into protected areas of forest in other parts of Brazil.

When there are only a few animals left, captive breeding may be the only way to save them from extinction.

This has been done with the Arabian oryx, a kind of desert antelope, which had been made extinct in the wild by hunting. In the early 1960's, the few remaining oryx were sent to a zoo in Arizona, USA, where they bred successfully. Some young antelopes were then sent back to Arabia, where they have settled in well. They are getting used to living wild.

Farming wildlife

Most wildlife at risk is found in the tropics, in the world's poorest countries. Here, most people are so poor and hungry that they can't afford to worry too much about wildlife. What you think of as wildlife, they think of as dinner!

The people with money often make things worse. People in Brazil are burning down rainforest to make way for cattle, to sell for hamburger meat to richer countries.

One way for both wildlife and people to survive is to farm wild animals. This has been tried out in the rainforest of Panama, Central America, with some big lizards called iguanas. Wild iguana's eggs are taken and hatched out, then the baby iguanas are kept until they are big enough to be let loose in the forest. They return to special places where food is left out for them, so they are easy to catch when they are ready to eat.

By ranching iguanas in the forest, you can get ten times as much meat than by burning the forest for cattle pasture. So in some places people are planting forest, where they were burning it down a few years ago.

Other animals that are farmed

Butterflies

Turtles

Crocodiles

Perhaps we will be eating iguana burgers one day.

A conservation success story

Rwanda is a small country in Africa, well known for its rare mountain gorillas. The gorillas have been on television, and thousands of tourists visit Rwanda every year to see them face to face.

Although they live in a national park, the gorillas have not always been safe. Poachers used to kill them and sell their heads to foreigners as trophies.

But the people of Rwanda now realise the gorillas are worth far more to them alive than dead.

The tourists who come to Rwanda spend a lot of money, which helps the people living there.

With a lot of help from people all over the world, the mountain gorillas now have a good chance of survival. But many other plants and animals around the world need the same kind of help if they are to survive, too.

How you can help

A bird's nesting box

Even when you know how wildlife is at risk all over the world, it is difficult to know how to help. One way is to support an organisation that helps wildlife, like the World Wide Fund for Nature. Friends of the Earth and Greenpeace are other organisations working for the world's wildlife.

A bird bath

A bird table

There is probably a nature organisation in your own town or county, that runs nature reserves. Ask your teacher to invite them to your school and tell your class about the local wildlife.

You can help wildlife in your own garden by digging out a pond. This gives frogs, toads and newts

Make sure you do something to help wildlife, even just a little, and encourage your friends to help too. Because now more than ever, wildlife needs all the friends it can get.

somewhere to lay their eggs – and makes a home for lots of other animals, too. You can put up nesting boxes for birds to breed in and you can grow plants which make food for birds, insects and colourful butterflies.

Wildlife Fact File

Rainforest destruction

Perhaps the worst danger ever for wildlife and for us is the destruction of the tropical rainforests in different parts of the world. It has been calculated that 100 acres of rainforest is destroyed every minute. This means that there are hundreds of animals and plants which are being destroyed at the same time. Some of these may well be kinds we know nothing about and may be helpful to us in some way. Some people think that one kind or species may become extinct every half hour.

Precious toads

Every year in spring groups of people in different parts of Europe go on a toad patrol. They help toads across roads so they will not get squashed by cars. This happens because toads move from where they hibernate over winter to the ponds where they will breed in the spring. In some countries special toad tunnels have been built under roads to allow the toads to move to their breeding ponds without even having to cross the road.

Not extinct!

Some animals which are thought to be extinct are sometimes rediscovered. Leadbeater's opposum and the parma wallaby from Australia were both rediscovered many years after they were thought to be extinct. When this happens, extra care is taken to make sure that the animals get the protection that they deserve.

The African violet

The African violet is often kept as a colourful house plant. These plants can be bought in shops. They have been specially grown for selling. But in the wild they are very rare. The last few wild African violet plants live on a mountain in Tanzania in Africa.

Endangered primate

The most seriously endangered species of primate (monkey or ape) is the golden lion marmoset. There are about 300 left in the wild. Of course through introducing these into the wild from zoo-bred animals numbers will increase eventually.

Turtle watch

The turtles which live in the sea are all in great danger. This is because the beaches where they lay their eggs are being destroyed. Hotels are being built there and tourists disturb the turtles preventing them from laying their eggs on the beach. Turtles are often hunted for food and for their shell which is used to make tortoiseshell products.

Endangered tortoises

Tortoises which were once commonly kept as pets are now protected in certain countries. For every tortoise which survived its journey to become a pet many others die. In the end tortoises were becoming quite rare. Today tortoises are not as common as pets, so they stand a better chance of surviving in the wild.

Poisonous seas

There is so much poisonous waste, such as chemicals being thrown into the world's seas, that in some parts of the sea the life there is dying. Some people think that these poisons cause fish, which people catch and eat, to become diseased and to die. Other animals, like seals, may be weakened by these poisons and they too may die.

Further information

There are many organisations involved with helping nature and our environment. Below are the addresses of just some of the more well known ones that you may like to contact. They may also be able to put you in touch with local organisations, if you want to get actively involved with things such as fund-raising through sponsored events. Remember, our natural world needs every friend and helper it can get!

Friends of the Earth
26-28 Underwood Street
London N1 7JQ

World Wide Fund for Nature
Panda House
Weyside Park
Godalming
Surrey GU7 1XR

British Trust for Nature Conservation
    Volunteers
36 St Mary's Street
Wallingford
Oxfordshire OX10 0EU

Greenpeace
30-31 Islington Green
London N1 8XT

The Conservation Trust
George Palmer Site
Northumberland Avenue
Reading
Berkshire RG2 7PW

Royal Society for the Protection of
    Birds
The Lodge
Sandy
Bedfordshire

The People's Trust for Endangered
    Species
Hamble house
Meadrow
Godalming
Surrey GU7 3JX

Glossary

Acid rain Rain that is mixed with polluting chemicals. It makes a weak acid and is harmful to plants and animals.

Cacti A type of plant that grows in deserts. They are usually thick stemmed and fleshy with prickles.

Crop Something that farmers grow on their land, like rice, wheat or corn.

Customs The place where people travelling to foreign countries are checked before they are allowed to enter.

Delicacy A tasty food. It is usually very difficult to find because it is rare and expensive.

Environment All the things in a particular area of land, including the animals, plants, hills, rocks, mountains, rivers and seas.

Extinct Something that does not exist anymore. The dinosaurs, for example, are extinct.

Habitat The natural surroundings of an animal or plant. The habitat of a cactus is the desert.

Illegal Something that is against the law. Stealing is illegal.

Medicine Something that people take to help cure a disease or sickness.

Poachers People who illegally catch or kill animals or plants and sell them to make money.

Pollution The things that make our world dirty and unsafe. People make a great deal of pollution (bad waste material).

Rainforest Forests that grow in the hot, rainy parts of the world. They have been called the world's lungs because they produce gases vital for people and animals to live.

Reptiles An animal that is cold-blooded, breathes air and is covered in scales.

Wetlands An area of land, usually close to sea level, that is very wet due to rivers, streams and ponds. Many animals and plants live in these areas.

Index